Rou✝e 66

Have you found your route in life?

Herbert I. Burns Jr.

To: Pastor. Alex

Route 66 – "Have you found your route in Life"
Copyright © 2019 by Herbert I Burns Jr.

ISBN 978-1-54397-835-3

Dedication

To my mom, Anna: for all of your love given to me and starting me on the right route.

To my wife, Susan: Thank you for coming into my life when I had strayed off the route. You are my angel and always will be.

To my sons Herbie and David: Thank you for the privilege of letting me to have been an influence on your route in life.

Table of Contents

Foreword
Gary D. Chapman

The Bible is the bestselling book in human history. Yet, many people have very limited knowledge of its content. They have never read it for themselves. Or, their reading has been sporadic and cursory. Route 66 is a unique tool for anyone who would like to get a better perspective on each of the 66 books of the Bible, and their implications for life.

The author's unique approach uses beautiful original digital paintings to capture one of the key messages in each book. Of course, each book of the Bible contains more than one topic, but the author focuses on the message that spoke most deeply to his own heart as he read and studied the book. The paintings reflect the creativity of God that dwells in the heart of every human. They also illustrate the old saying, "one picture is worth a thousand words."

However, with each painting there are words. The brief devotionals which accompany each painting lead the reader to apply the message behind the painting to their own life. Challenges to pray, help someone, thank someone, and examine your own words and actions will make this book more than an academic exercise.

Parents will find this book helpful in exposing their children to the basic teachings of the Bible. The paintings will provoke thought in the mind of a child. Questions like, "Mom, what does this picture mean?" will offer opportunities to dialogue with your children. Even teenagers will find this book interesting and challenging.

I don't know of another book that connects people with the Bible by use of beautiful digital paintings and real-world application. I predict that Route 66 will be a legacy book passed from generation to generation.

Gary D. Chapman, Ph.D. author of "The 5 Love Languages"

Introduction

Has your navigation system ever gone out, and you were lost on your route? Route 66 can put you back on the correct route. We all want to reach our final destination, and certainly, our heavenly destination.

I was relying on my own navigation system, not God's. When I realized I was lost, I sent out a distress signal.

So begins the story. I finally reached a time that I needed to stop asking God "What can You do for me?" but "God, what can I do for You?" This was spurred on by a series of events in my life where I was trying to achieve on my own and was failing! Finally, I said, "God, I am giving this up! I release myself to You, and if it's Your will, it will be done. I must put my trust in You". It was at that point I said to myself, "I am not going to pursue this route anymore, and I will not continue these efforts with what I am trying to achieve."

Then surprisingly, God's navigation system was engaged, and His route led me to discover how to use my talents to spread his Word.

You can discover how to use your talents also. He opened the door for me, and I walked through. Now I have prepared the first door for you to open. Turn to page 12 and begin to find your route in life. Prayerfully, when you have finished this book, the journey will be life-changing! Then share your experiences from this book with others that they also might find their route in life.

Colossians 3:23
"Whatever you do, work at it with all your heart, as working for the Lord, not for men."

BOOK 1 Genesis
Context:

Welcome to the beginning of your route. Genesis has many examples of disobedience to God. First Adam and Eve, then the people, and the great flood that followed, etc.... But there was one who trusted and obeyed, and that was Abraham. He stood out to me. Continue to read about his incredible trust and obedience.

Genesis 22 v2 "Then God said, take your son, your only son, whom you love—Isaac—and go to the region of Moriah. Sacrifice him there as a burnt offering on a mountain I will show you." v12 "Do not lay a hand on the boy," He said. "Do not do anything to him. Now I know that you fear God, because you have not withheld from Me your son, your only son. v13 Abraham looked up and there in a thicket he saw a ram caught by its horns. He went over and took the ram and sacrificed it as a burnt offering instead of his son. v14 So Abraham called that place The Lord Will Provide. And to this day it is said, "On the mountain of the Lord it will be provided."

Application:

What have you sacrificed? What would you sacrifice if God asked you? Having lost a son unexpectedly and living with that loss, I cannot begin to imagine the trust Abraham had in God. We must have that same trust in Him daily. What would God have me do? What would God have you do? We must be in communication with God. We must be still, listen, and **trust and obey His words** in our applications to daily life. Find a Bible and read the beginning of creation as told in Genesis. Amazing, just amazing!

Illustration 1- Abraham and Isaac Embrace after God Provided a Sacrifice

BOOK 2 Exodus
Context:

Exodus 16 v3 "If only we had died by the Lord's hand in Egypt! There we sat around pots of meat and ate all the food we wanted, but you have brought us out into this desert to starve this entire assembly to death. v4 Then the Lord said to Moses, I will rain down bread from heaven for you. The people are to go out each day and gather enough for that day. In this way I will test them and see whether they will follow My instructions."

Application:

Just imagine. God provided food for hundreds of thousands of Israelites for 40 years, testing them to see if they would follow His instructions. Has God provided for you? I think that if you look closely at your life you might find times that God has provided for you. Take a look back into your life. Perhaps it was a job, your spouse, your children, medical healing, or some other God-driven event. There is one event in my life I will never forget! At the time, my wife and I and our two children were in a position where we had no money left to buy food for our family until the next payday (which was in two weeks). To the best of our knowledge no one knew of our financial situation. We had faith that God would provide somehow and prayed about it. It was either that afternoon or the next day that the associate pastor of our church came by and said that there was someone who wanted to remain anonymous, and who wanted us to have this $100 bill. Through our trust in God, He provided. God will provide in His own time and own way. God provided for us. **We should ask God how we can provide for others.**

Illustration 2 - Hands of Plenty

BOOK 3 Leviticus
Context:

Leviticus 19 v9 "I am the Lord your God. v11 "Do not steal. Do not lie. Do not deceive one another. v12 Do not swear falsely by My Name and so profane the Name of your God. I am the Lord. v13 Do not defraud or rob your neighbor. Do not hold back the wages of a hired worker overnight. v14 Do not curse the deaf or put a stumbling block in front of the blind but fear your God. I am the Lord. v15 Do not pervert justice; do not show partiality to the poor or favoritism to the great but judge your neighbor fairly." v37 "Keep all My decrees and all My laws and follow them."

I am the Lord." Please take time to read all of the laws in Leviticus 19. If I included them all, there would not be room for the application on this page.

Application:

While we don't have to make a sacrifice for our sins because our Lord and Savior did this for us, we still have to respect the laws of man, and we should also respect the laws of God. Have you ever spoken ill of someone, have you ever taken something that wasn't yours, and have you coveted what others have? I have. We all are sinners; we should try, to the best of our abilities, to obey God's laws and be examples for others. God is always watching. Others may be watching also, and you might be that Godly example when others see you taking the higher ground and doing the right godly things. Someone once said, "It's the little things in life that matter." Those little things done for God's glory just might turn out to be a huge thing in someone's life. **What can you do to be an example for God?**

LEVITICUS

Illustration 3 - The Scrolls of Justice, the Flames of Sacrifice, and the Stones of Punishment

BOOK 4 Numbers
Context:

Numbers 20 v7 "The Lord said to Moses, v8 Take the staff, and you and your brother Aaron gather the assembly together. Speak to that rock before their eyes and it will pour out its water. You will bring water out of the rock for the community so they and their livestock can drink. v9 So Moses took the staff from the Lord's presence, just as He commanded him. v10 He and Aaron gathered the assembly together in front of the rock and Moses said to them, "Listen, you rebels, must we bring you water out of this rock?" v11 Then Moses raised his arm and struck the rock twice with his staff. Water gushed out."

Application:

Have you ever witnessed what you would consider a miracle? There are many miracles in my life but let me share one with you. Recently my wife excitedly said, "Hurry to the deck and look!" When I came, there was a large rainbow emanating from the ground in our yard going straight up in a heavenly direction, parallel to the stair tower at our house. It hadn't rained!

Just inside of that stair tower hanging on the wall was a painting our son David had done of the nativity and one of the crucifixions. The connection was truly amazing! I ran to get the camera, but the rainbow disappeared as quickly as it appeared. **Take the time to look as miracles are all around you.** A rainbow, the birth of a child, someone cured from illness, the rain, the sun, the moon, and the stars: all miracles. And yes, you are a miracle, a creation made in God's image, with a special purpose in life, according to God's marvelous plan.

NUMBERS

Illustration 4 - From this Rock the Water Came

BOOK 5 Deuteronomy
Context:

Deuteronomy 3 v23 "At that time, too, I entreated the Lord, saying: v24 O Lord God, You have only begun to show your servant your greatness and your might; what god in heaven or on earth can perform deeds and mighty acts like yours! v25 Let me cross over to see the good land beyond the Jordan, that good hill country and the Lebanon. v26 But the Lord was angry with me on your account and would not heed me. The Lord said to me, "Enough from you! Never speak to me of this matter again! v27 Go up to the top of Pisgah and look around you to the west, to the north, to the south, and to the east. Look well, for you shall not cross over this Jordan."

Application:

We should be careful how we respond to what God wants for us, and what He asks us to do. God denied Moses access to the promised land for his disobedience. God has a promised land for us, Heaven.

Do you have an earthly Canaan (a promised place or region for you to live and prosper)? Can you leave behind your broken life? Have you been in bondage because of lust for money, sex, or materials things?

Perhaps your life has been fragmented because of your ego. I have experienced some of those things. When I started to ask "God, what can I do for You" rather than "God, what can You do for me", I could begin to see my earthly Canaan as a place where we are connected, where life is more rich through Him and with Him, and where life is more fulfilling. **Is life all about Him or me?**

DEUTERONOMY

Illustration 5 - Moses Looking to the Promised Land

BOOK 6 Joshua
Context:

Joshua 6 v1 "Now the gates of Jericho were securely barred because of the Israelites. No one went out and no one came in. v2 Then the Lord said to Joshua, "See, I have delivered Jericho into your hands, along with its king and its fighting men. v3 March around the city once with all the armed men. Do this for six days. v4 Have seven priests carry trumpets of rams' horns in front of the ark. On the seventh day, march around the city seven times, with the priests blowing the trumpets. v5 When you hear them sound a long blast on the trumpets, have the whole army give a loud shout; then the wall of the city will collapse and the army will go up, everyone straight in."

Application:

In your life have you ever encountered what seems to be an impenetrable fortress preventing you to succeed? Remember with faithful purpose, how God intervened for the Israelites at Jericho.

In my life there was a time when I was trying to achieve something that would have created profound recognition in my profession. Well, I failed, and I failed again. At this point after two years of work I said, "Lord, it's not Your will. I submit, to You." I prayed and asked, "What would You have me do?" A year later, I received an unsolicited request to try again. Well! I became the first person in my family to be a Fulbright Scholar to the Russian Federation.

So, if there are barriers in your life, **take your heart to the Lord, and pray for His will to be done, not yours**. Accept the outcomes. I have discovered that God does things in His own way and His own time.

JOSHUA

Illustration 6 - The Walls Came Tumbling Down

BOOK 7 Judges
Context:

Judges 1 v1 "Now after the death of Joshua it came to pass, that the children of Israel asked the Lord, saying, who shall go up for us against the Canaanites first, to fight against them? v2 And the Lord said, Judah shall go up..."

This cycle of leadership, sin, and forgiveness lasted for 319 years as God continued to forgive the Israelites and lift up successive judges to serve the people. The judges where Othniel, Ehud, Shamgar, Deborah, Gideon, Tola, Jair, Jephthah, Ibzan, Elon, Abdon, and Samson.

Application:

When we reflect on the people of America since our founding in 1776, our nation now being 242 years old, who comes to mind as Godly leaders of this nation?
George Washington, John Adams, Jefferson, Lincoln, Cleveland, Eisenhower, or our current President? What about nonpolitical leaders? Jonathon Edwards, Charles Spurgeon, Martin Luther King, Jr., Billy Graham, T.D. Jakes, just to name a few.

We know that God is our ultimate Spiritual Leader through Jesus Christ our Savior, but you have an earthly spiritual leader that you look to as a man of God?
Someone that you can look to as a shining example of how we as Christians should respond to and follow the gospel? I have several. **Find someone that is your spiritual leader if you have not.** Your life can be changed forever.

JUDGES

Illustration 7 - The Twelve Judges

BOOK 8 Ruth
Context:

Ruth 4 v13 "So Boaz took Ruth, and she became his wife. And he went into her, and the Lord gave her conception, and she bore a son. v14 Then the women said to Naomi, "Blessed be the Lord, who has not left you this day without a redeemer, and may his name be renowned in Israel! v15 He shall be to you a restorer of life and a nourisher of your old age, for your daughter-in-law who loves you, who is more to you than seven sons, has given birth to him."

Application:

The book of Ruth is really a story of loyalty and love. Ruth stayed with Naomi through terrible hardship. We belong to a God who is faithful, loving, and a powerful God Who provides for His children. In times of terrible hardship, are you willing to stay the course with someone, perhaps in a marriage or a business partnership? I recall the story told to me by General Norman Gaddis at a lunch many years ago. The title of his presentation was "My five Christmases in Captivity". Norman was a POW in Vietnam during the war. He shared about routine torture and mistreatment from his captors. Through it all, he stayed the course and shared God's words with his fellow prisoners by tapping in Morse code on the prison walls. Norman maintained his honor to our country and his faith in God.

Can you keep your faith in God's goodness with knowledge that we are called to respond to that divine grace in faithful obedience, in spite of the godless culture in which we might live? The reward for Ruth was the lineage of Christ! You can stay the course! **You can be strong!**

RUTH

Illustration 8 - Naomi and Ruth Just Surviving

BOOK 9 1st Samuel
Context:

1st Samuel 16 v7 "But the LORD said unto Samuel, "Look not on his countenance, or on the height of his stature; because I have refused him: for the LORD seeth not as man seeth; for man looketh on the outward appearance, but the LORD looketh on the heart." v19 "Wherefore Saul sent messengers unto Jesse, and said, "Send me David thy son, which is with the sheep."

Application:

When Saul sent for David, he didn't know that David was anointed to be the future king. and that David would later be "King of Israel".

When we meet people for the first time, we may know a little about them, but we really don't truly know what is in their heart and what they might become one day. A king, a president, a pastor, a great father or mother, a leader in another field? My application is to **treat everyone** we might meet in the business world, family, or friends **with respect** and honor, for we don't truly know their heart or understand all of their talents, and what greatness they might achieve one day.

I SAMUEL

Illustration 9 - David Soothing King Saul

BOOK 10 2nd Samuel
Context:

2nd Samuel 22 v1 "And David spake unto the Lord the words of this song in the day that the Lord had delivered him out of the hand of all his enemies, and out of the hand of Saul."

Please take the time to read the song of David. The verses were too long to include on this page. What a joyful read this will be!

Find a Bible, and turn to 2nd Samuel 22, and read v2-51.

Application:

Anyone can fail, even if they are blessed by GOD, just as King David did. We must protect our minds and hearts, so as not to wander. We must remain humble, not prideful, and resist temptation of ungodly thoughts and actions. Isn't it much better to do the right things in life rather than to ask forgiveness after our sinful actions?

Let me challenge you to look heavenward, outstretch your arms, and sing praise to God for your blessings and His forgiveness of your sins. **Ask God to show you what you can do for Him.** Then be still and listen and look for His signs in the future for you. What better time than now to discover your conversation with God!

Illustration 10 - David's Song to God

BOOK 11 1st Kings
Context:

At the end of King David's reign, Solomon was anointed king, and he did right in his youth. He was faithful to God and built the temple. No one's wisdom matched his. Then as he aged, he became evil, taking many wives of different religions, and worshiping their idols.

This was the beginning of the downfall of Israel. After Solomon, there were thirty-nine kings of which only five are recognized as godly Kings (or good kings). The nation was split into Israel and Judah, with all their succession of kings, which led to a weakened body in God. That led eventually to the destruction of the temple and the people being taken into captivity by the Babylonians. The illustration represents the crowns of all the fallen kings during this time and the lost souls of God (a fallen people).

Application:

Look at the illustration. Contemplate during your life, the kings and rulers of nations and peoples that have also been led astray. Can you consider what has happened to the cultures in Germany, Africa, the Middle East and elsewhere?

Is our nation drifting away from God? What can we do about it? What can you do about it? It's important to be faithful to God and to share the Words of Christ with others. If we don't who will? Let's not let our generation look back and see all of the lost crowns and opportunities missed that unite us with God and Jesus Christ. **You can be a political force for change** through action and prayer.

I KINGS

Illustration 11 - The Crowns of Judah and Israel

BOOK 12 2nd Kings
Context:

2nd Kings 24 v11 "And Nebuchadnezzar king of Babylon came against the city, and his servants did besiege it. v12 and Jehoiachin the king of Judah went out to the king of Babylon, he, and his mother, and his servants, and his princes, and his officers: and the king of Babylon took him in the eighth year of his reign. v13 And he carried out thence all the treasures of the house of the LORD, and the treasures of the king's house, and cut in pieces all the vessels of gold which Solomon king of Israel had made in the temple of the LORD. v14 And he carried away all Jerusalem, and all the princes, and all the mighty men of valor, even ten thousand captives, and all the craftsmen and smiths: none remained, save the poorest sort of the people of the land. v15 And he carried away Jehoiachin to Babylon, and the king's mother, and the king's wives, and his officers, and the mighty of the land, those carried he into captivity from Jerusalem to Babylon."

Application:

Just like the people of Jerusalem, if we wander away from God, the devil could hold us captive. Our sinful actions could result in loss of property, money, and family. We can be held in captive for many years as a result of our actions. Keep your eye on God and your faith as a Christian and never fear being taken captive. God is my eternal freedom and yours. **Don't wander away from your route in life.**

Illustration 12 - Captives of Jerusalem by King Nebuchadnezzar

BOOK 13 1st Chronicles
Context:

Upon returning from captivity, the Jews were returning to a land that was once theirs and was now in poverty.

They possessed little from the former kingdom. To begin again, they had to turn to the face of God and away from the pain and evil that caused their captivity. One such man was Jabez, and he turned his face to God and prayed this prayer.

Prayer of Jabez

1st Chronicles 4 v10 "And Jabez called on the God of Israel, saying, oh that Thou wouldest bless me indeed, and enlarge my coast, and that Thine Hand might be with me, and that Thou wouldest keep me from evil, that it may not grieve me! And God granted him that which he requested."

Application:

How often do we pray and what do we pray for?

Honestly, I need to pray more than I have. I need to be in communication with God more. If you don't pray much, the prayer of Jabez could be a good start. Pray that God will expand your territory. Pray that He will keep you from evil. Pray that He will bring no harm to you. While you are praying this prayer, also ask what can you do to expand God's territory. Pray that you can lead others from evil.

You can start right now. Just close your eyes, put your hands together, be sincere, and **speak from your heart to God.** What a wonderful thing this is to do!

I CHRONICLES

Illustration 13- Prayer of Jabez

BOOK 14 2nd Chronicles
Context:

After returning from captivity where the Jews served kings that worshiped idols, they upheld the faith of David and prospered.

2 Chronicles 7 v14 "If My people who are called by My name will humble themselves, and pray and seek My face, and turn from their wicked ways, then I will hear from heaven, and will forgive their sin and heal their land."

2 Chronicles 24 v18 "They abandoned the house of the LORD, the God of their fathers, and served the Asherim and the idols; so, wrath came upon Judah and Jerusalem for this their guilt."

Application:

In reflection, after reading 2nd Chronicles, the big story is the building of the temple by Solomon; the retelling of the story of the kings, those who walked in God's grace, and those that abandoned God. For me, the greatest take-aways are the choices to either be full in the life by living in the Spirit that God wants for us, or to abandon God and be barren and without.

The illustration represents the revelation that I want to be full of the Spirit in life and not barren, without His life or Spirit. The choice is easy to make. Consider where you are? Think about the choice you might make. Earthly life is short. **Don't wait too long.**

II CHRONICLES

Illustration 14 - Full of Life or Barren

BOOK 15 Ezra

Context:

King Cyrus, who became in the favor of God, decreed that those willing return to Jerusalem should rebuild the temple according to Gods commands. The first contingent included Zerubbabel, and he began reconstruction.

But there where those that opposed and petitioned Artaxerxes to have work stopped. Later Darius found the decree from King Cyrus and he declared that work continue. King Artaxerxes was moved by God to commission Ezra to reestablish the Law of God, and to appoint magistrates to govern over all the people and inform them of the laws of God.

Application:

Do you know of a pastor or priest of a church that has been called to bring order back into God's house? There may be peoples of the church or congregation that try to delay or interfere with the works of God. Their concern is for themselves, not the church. Look inward, should you be in a situation like this. Pray that you can support God's chosen pastor or priest. Don't be the thorn like those who tried to stop the remnant of Israel from the rebuilding of Solomon's temple. In business, have you been in a situation where you are brought in to rebuild an organization? Are there people that want to disrupt your efforts? Stay true to the course. Stay true to your principles. Become the leader that you can be in order to bring rebuilding and stability to your mission. Learn from those experiences and become an instrument for others to learn from you. **The more you give with godly intentions, the more you will be blessed.**

EZRA

Illustration 15 - Zerubbabel Instructing Workers on the Rebuilding of Solomon's Temple

BOOK 16 Nehemiah
Context:

Nehemiah was the cup bearer to King Artaxerxes. This meant that he tasted the wine first to see if there was no poison in it before it was given to the king. Nehemiah heard about the destruction and despair in Jerusalem. Nehemiah 1 v3 "And they said unto me, "The remnant that are left of the captivity there in the province are in great affliction"... "when he heard these words, he sat down and wept, and mourned, and fasted, and prayed before the God of heaven."

When serving wine to King Artaxerxes, the king noticed that Nehemiah was troubled, and he told the king of his prayer to restore Jerusalem. The king was so moved, he sent him on his journey to restore the city, the people, and their relationships with their God and Savior. Nehemiah was a servant to the king and became a servant to God.

Application:

Are you in a situation where your work has become the king that you serve? Are you not putting God first? Follow your heart and seek God's guidance and look for His answers. Nehemiah left his job for another because he wanted to be obedient to God. Do you need to leave your job? Do you need to have a new vision for your job? Who are you serving? When you are on the right route be ready to deal with those who oppose you. **You must be determined to see your vision through.** Remember your future is worth fighting for, and never forget that God has a vision for us. He is our Potter, and He is never finished with us until we reach Heaven.

NEHEMIAH

Illustration 16 - Nehemiah Preparing to Serve the King

BOOK 17 Esther
Context:

Esther 5 v9 "Then went Haman forth that day joyful and with a glad heart: but when Haman saw Mordecai in the king's gate, that he stood not up, nor moved for him, he was full of indignation against Mordecai. When he returned home, he had a feast with his wife and friends, and was boastful about all of the glory and riches the king was promising him and his family and servants. His wife was angry that Mordecai did not recognize her husband as royalty." v14 "Then said Zeresh his wife and all his friends unto him, let gallows be made of fifty cubits high, and tomorrow speak thou unto the king that Mordecai may be hanged thereon: then go thou in merrily with the king unto the banquet. And the thing pleased Haman; and he caused the gallows to be made."

Application:

Our application in life is to beware of pride. Haman's pride was causing the destruction of others. Beware of pride in your life. "Pride comes before a fall". God will humble us, and then we will fail if we do not see the errors of our ways.

Pride led to the destruction of Haman and his family (Haman was sent to the gallows instead). Be careful when you demand the consideration and respect from others, and their agreements with your views. Check out your views and see if they are spiritually aligned. "Humble yourself before the Lord." Your view will then have a stronger faithful foundation. **Discover humility**.

ESTHER

Illustration 17 - The King with Esther Sending Haman to the Gallows He had Prepared for Mordecai (His pride led to his destruction).

BOOK 18 Job
Context:

God was challenged by Satan that He could prove that Job would lose faith in Him if his possessions were taken away. God removed all of Job's property, his children died, and he remained faithful to God.

On one day Job lost everything, and his response was: Job 1 v2 "And he said, Naked came I out of my mother's womb, and naked shall I return thither: the LORD gave, and the LORD hath taken away; blessed be the Name of the LORD."

God pointed out that Job was still a man of faith. Satan then said to destroy Job's flesh and he will surely lose faith. Satan then smote Job with sore boils from the sole of his foot unto his crown. Job lost friends, was accused of sinning, and this was his punishment.

In the end Job prevailed: Job 22 v23 "If thou return to the Almighty, thou shalt be built up, thou shalt put away iniquity far from thy tabernacles." God returned Job to health and restored and multiplied his belongings. (Find a Bible and read this amazing story of faith)

Application:

Remember that bad things can happen to good people. Can you recall a time of terrible tragedy? Friends and circumstances may fail us, but God never does. Remember that God is in control, and we should keep faith in times of trouble. Trouble in life is not necessarily punishment for our sins. God is always listening, and we must trust that He hears and always cares. **Be faithful.**

Illustration 18 - Eliphaz, the Temanite, Bildad, the Shuhite, and Zophar, the Naamathite, Confront Job

BOOK 19 Psalms
Context:

Psalms is a collection of lyrical poems, hymns, prayers, and songs of praise. The writing of Psalms spans a time of about 1,000 years. Contributors include Moses, David, Asaph, and Solomon. David wrote some of the Psalms that give thanks to the trials and test during his life (always praising God).

My favorite is Psalm 23 v1-6. "The Lord is my shepherd; I shall not want. He maketh me to lie down in green pastures: He leadeth me beside the still waters. He restoreth my soul: He leadeth me in the paths of righteousness for His name's sake. Yea, though I walk through the valley of the shadow of death, I will fear no evil: for Thou art with me; Thy rod and Thy staff they comfort me. Thou preparest a table before me in the presence of mine enemies: Thou anointest my head with oil; my cup runneth over. Surely goodness and mercy shall follow me all the days of my life: and I will dwell in the House of the Lord forever."

Application:

Keep your faith in God. He will: Restore you; lead you; protect you: comfort you; give you peace: give you strength; give you rest. Sing God's blessings whenever you can. Thank God for your blessings and opportunities often. Let your light be a beacon for others to see. Believe me, they will see that beacon in you. One year on a trip to the Republic of Belarus someone said to me "Why are you always happy and smiling?" My response was, "Because the Lord is with me." **Take the Lord with you and be joyful.**

PSALMS

Illustration 19 - Symbolic Representation of Psalms 23

BOOK 20 Proverbs
Context:

Proverbs were primarily written by King Solomon. God told Solomon He would grant him whatever he requested, and his request was not for money or fame, but for discernment. This led him to be the wisest of God's chosen. Most of the writings where completed between 970 and 930 BC. These proverbs serve as a guide to offer wisdom and understanding regarding judgement in life with lessons and knowledge for all ages. There are so many lessons to learn1 Let me encourage you to find a Bible and begin reading Proverbs.

Application:

Wow! What a book this is! So much wisdom to share with the young and old. These instructions and comments recorded in Proverbs are timeless and cover many areas of life such as anger, children, education, law, marriage, work, just to mention a few. I wish that these wisdoms could appear more in our educational systems for life preparations. I do have a couple favorites: Proverbs 25 v19 "As water reflects the face, so one's life reflects the heart." Our life can be a beacon to others and Proverbs 13 v20 says, "He that walketh with wise men shall be wise: but a companion of fools shall be destroyed."

Choose carefully those you associate with as you could become more like them. As you read through Proverbs, use this knowledge for yourself, but more importantly, share these wisdoms with others, that they will be on the right route in life.

Illustration 20 - Never too Old to Learn

BOOK 21 Ecclesiastes
Context:

It is said that Ecclesiastes was possibly written by a Qoheleth which is referred to as the "Preacher" or "Teacher", or someone who calls together an assembly or addresses an assembly. Scholars believe that Solomon is responsible for the writings because it is mentioned that no one else was the "son of David". This book refers to a time of reflection in the life of Solomon. Ecclesiastes 7 v14 "When times are good, be happy; but when times are bad, consider this: God has made the one as well as the other."

Application:

Make the most of life in the correct way. Time cannot be reclaimed; time cannot be captured. We live in the moment, we remember the past, and we look forward to the future. Be careful that your vanity, pride, and wants don't cause harm to others, or that your wisdom causes others to suffer wrongly. Remember you have had successes and failures, and there will be future successes and failures.

Ecclesiastes 3 v1 "There is a time for everything, and a season for every activity under the heavens."

We will not be measured by what we have done over time. We will be judged on how well we have kept His commandments. We should try to live our lives with God's purposes in mind. God is still molding us. **Let us be sure that the clay is the best we can provide Him** so that when we are at the end of our time He might say "You have done well, my good and faithful servant."

ECCLESIASTES

Illustration 21 - "There is a time for everything, and a season for every activity under the heavens."

BOOK 22 Song of Solomon
Context:

Solomon probably wrote this in the early years of his reign. The time is speculated at around 965 BC. These songs are to praise the virtues of a relationship between a husband and his wife. While there is no mention of God in the Song of Solomon some translators see this as a symbolic relationship of Christ and His church. Christ is seen as the king as Solomon was. The church is represented as his wife, the Shulamite. While the Song of Solomon is a literal description of marriage, the allegory of Christ and His care for His bride, the church, must also be considered.

Application:

Put into perspective the power of love. To quote from the movie Les Misérables, "And remember, as it was written, to love another person is to see the face of God." The musician and vocalist, Themis Tolis, said, "To love is nothing. To be loved is something. But to love and be loved, that's everything." So it is, with our relationship with God and our spouse. God loves us unconditionally, as we should also love. **Give your spouse the necessary attention, encouragement and praise they need.** Who wants to always hear criticism? Enjoy each other and do things together. Work through problems. One thing my wife and I do is to never let the sun set on our anger. Do whatever is necessary to reconnect that love before the sun sets if you are serious about love. If you need additional readings about this, one great source might be The Five Love Languages, written by Dr. Gary Chapman. But remember, God will bring us to the banqueting house, and His banner over us is love!

SONG OF SOLOMON

Illustration 22 - "His left hand is under my head, and His right hand embraces me!" Song of Solomon 2 v6

BOOK 23 Isaiah
Context:

Isaiah is the accounting of one of God's prophets, and his writings were around 720 BC. There are two distinct parts of the writings. First is his encounter with God and the prophecy of problems, both ethical and political in Judah, corruption, and that God can save His people from further destruction. Next is the prophecy: Isaiah 7 v14 "Therefore the Lord Himself shall give you a sign; Behold, a virgin shall conceive, and bear a Son, and shall call His name Immanuel. Isaiah 9 v6 "For unto us a child is born, unto us a Son is given, and the government shall be upon His shoulder: and his name shall be called Wonderful, Counselor, The mighty God, The everlasting Father, The Prince of Peace."

Application:

Can you imagine seeing God, let alone having a conversation with Him? If this happened to you or me, who would believe us in our generation, let alone listen and act on what He told us.

If you go back to the first illustration in this book the only plaque to have a subtitle is this one, **"Trust and Obey".** It is hard sometimes for us to stay on our route in life, but we must "trust and obey for there is no other way." If we can stay the course and are true to the Christian beliefs, our rewards will be more than anything here on earth. Isaiah26 v4 "Trust ye in the LORD forever: for in the LORD JEHOVAH is everlasting strength."

We need to have eyes that see and ears that listen and minds that respond to these purposes in life here on earth.

Illustration 23 - "I saw also the Lord sitting upon a throne, high and lifted up..." Isaiah 6 v1

BOOK 24 Jeremiah

Context:

Jeremiah was approximately 16 when he received Words directly from God. God instructed Jeremiah to reveal several prophecies to the Israelites. (Jeremiah was about 20 years old when he began sharing the prophecies). These included the warning of the destruction of Judah if Judah did not a return to God, protection of the remnant, and destruction of the King and later restoration of Judah.

Jeremiah's prophecies were rejected by the priests and prophets. He was imprisoned, released, imprisoned again, and put in a pit, but God said that He would protect him. Then he was taken from the pit and locked in a cell. Later, after the destruction of Jerusalem, Jeremiah was released from prison by the orders of King Nebuchadnezzar.

Application:

Jeremiah 22 v29 "O earth, earth, earth, hear the word of the LORD." The words of Jeremiah fell on deaf ears. Are our ears deaf today? What truth will spur us to follow God? Just look around. Is our civilization acting like Jerusalem did? God is patient with us and ready for us to love Him and be loved by Him. We should be smart enough to know good from evil and to know when we are disobedient in regard to our loved ones, family, and friends.

Can you or I be a part of a reformation who tell others and become beacons to spread His Word, love, and joy? Yes, we can rely on God, and He will respond.

Do good in His eyes for the right reasons. **What will you choose to do?**

JEREMIAH

Illustration 24 - Rejection by the Priests Concerning the Prophecies from God as Spoken by Jeremiah

BOOK 25 Lamentations
Context:

The prophecies of God that were spoken by Jeremiah came true. The city of Jerusalem was conquered by the Babylonians. They set the city on fire and destroyed it. They also took the officials, men, women, and children, and left the desolate in the city. There was no food, and many starved. Some even ate their children to survive. The king of Babylon, knowing about the prophecies of Jeremiah, made him afraid to harm this man of God, so he had him released from captivity and set him loose in the city. Jeremiah saw all the destruction and was devastated by the wrath of God. Jeremiah cries out and laments in sorrow. He knows that God is faithful and steadfast in His love, and that God has said that He will protect the remnant, and it will start anew in seventy years. From these ashes, a new foundation will arise, and Jeremiah will continue to share God's Words.

Application:

Try to relate this to all the suffering that takes place today; all of the deaths caused by war, abortions, and domestic violence. All of these things make us cry out and lament. We must have hope in God to turn things around. We can continue to hope and cry out! Remember that through suffering strength of character can come. I pray that no one has to suffer but I know it will happen. Just remember to keep your faith and trust in God as He is our Savior and can ease the suffering. If you have seen tragedy. **Trust in God** and be transformed from the pain.

LAMENTATIONS

Illustration 25 - "For these things I weep; mine eye, mine eye runneth down with water." Lamentations 1 v16

BOOK 26 Ezekiel
Context:

Ezekiel was taken into captivity about 586 BC and later became a prophet. God continually asked him during the many years of captivity to speak of repentance to the people and return to God. During this time, Ezekiel also received six visions:

- The first was the prophetic vision of the Throne of Heaven (first apocalyptic vision in the Bible)
- The first "temple vision"
- "Vision of Israel"
- The vision of "The valley of dry bones"
- The vision of the destruction of Gog and Magog
- The final "temple vision"

It is believed that Ezekiel was 25 when he was exiled, about 30 when he received his first vision, and 52 by the time of his last vision. Make time to read the visions in Ezekiel.

Application:

Be aware of your surroundings, look and listen, and be in tune to what God wants for you. Don't be influenced by the world. Be an influencer! Go where you are called to go. Do not be fearful to influence others with God's Words. This is what He asks us. Go out and make a difference in someone's life, your community, your nation, or the world. Without God we are nothing. As Christians we are responsible for sharing the Gospel with others.

God can restore us! He can breathe life into us just as He did in the valley of dry bones. Without it, we are just empty bodies like dry bones. We do have a purpose beyond just simply existing. Please pray to seek your purpose and **ask for God's guidance in your route in life.**

EZEKIEL

Illustration 26 - "I will cause breath to enter into you and you shall live...you shall know that I am the Lord." Ezekiel 37 v6

BOOK 27 Daniel
Context:

The book of Daniel takes place between 560-536 B.C. Daniel was taken into captivity by King Nebuchadnezzar along with Shadrach, Meshach, and Abednego. They were taken because of their intellect and beauty. Daniel translates the king's dream and is appointed to high service for the king. Daniel's friends, Shadrach, Meshach, and Abednego are thrown into a fiery furnace for not bowing down to an idol. King Nebuchadnezzar, who sees God in the furnace, is moved to believe briefly in God, but returns to his idol worship.

Daniel predicts the destruction of the king and the king is overthrown. The new king, Darius, appoints Daniel to high authority. Jealous rivals create a plot to have Daniel killed because of his praying against the commandment of the king. Daniel is thrown into the den of lions, but an angel saves him. The king sees the power of God and then throws the accusers into the lions' den and restores Daniel to his authority. Daniel has a series of additional visions. Read the book of Daniel to discover these.

Application:

Be strong and truthful and have courage. Don't tell someone what you think they want to hear. **Stand on your Christian principals regardless of the outcome.** In today's world, it seems that we want to be politically correct rather than correct. When Daniel was thrown into the lions' den, his faith saved him. He was not eaten. Think of all of the Christians in these times who have lost their lives because of their faith but remember that they are still saved.

DANIEL

Illustration 27- Daniel is Saved from Lions' Den

BOOK 28 Hosea
Context:

The book of Hosea is written between 750-722 BC. This is the recording of the messages as written by Hosea.

This is a time that God's relationship with Israel includes judgement, but on the other side of this relationship, God remains faithful. God advises Hosea to marry a person of whoredom which becomes a symbol of the relationship of God and the people of Israel (symbolic as God's wife or bride). Hosea continues to deliver the message to those who have sinned admonishing them to return to the ways of God, but they don't. Gomer continues to be unfaithful, leaves Hosea, and later is sold into slavery. Hosea finds out, and God again commands him to love Gomer just as He loves his chosen remnant.

Application:

Have you forgiven those who were once under your judgement? Are there problems in your marriage that need forgiveness and restoration through love? As we continue our route through the Bible, we can read in 1st Corinthians 13 v7 where we read "Love bears all things, believes all things, hopes all things, endures all things." This is the case for Hosea. This is the case for God and us. This is the case for you and me in our relationships. Give love and hope to your spouse and give God a chance.

Is there someone your need to love or forgive? **Don't wait!**

Illustration 28 - Gomer as a Slave Being Sold Back to Hosea

BOOK 29 Joel
Context:

It is difficult to place exact dates on the book of Joel, but most scholars suspect that the writings took place around 835 BC. Joel continues to share God's words to the remnant, the majority not listening, and are still lusting, drinking, and worshiping other gods. God's message is stern but there is still hope for repentance. My illustration for this book of the Bible is based on the following passages:

Joel 2 v1 "Blow ye the trumpet in Zion and sound an alarm in my holy mountain: let all the inhabitants of the land tremble: v31 "The sun shall be turned into darkness, and the moon into blood, before the great and the terrible day of the LORD comes. v32 It shall come to pass, that whosoever shall call on the name of the LORD shall be delivered: for in Mount Zion and in Jerusalem shall be deliverance, as the LORD hath said, and in the remnant whom the LORD shall call." Joel 3 v16 "The LORD also shall roar out of Zion and utter His voice from Jerusalem; and the heavens and the earth shall shake but the LORD will be the hope of His people, and the strength of the children of Israel."

Application:

During my life there have been difficult, trying, and dangerous times. God uses these experiences to strengthen our trust in Him by strengthening our faith in Him. I survived these trials. The day is coming, and I want to be ready. It is through salvation we escape the ultimate wrath. Do you have problems and need forgiveness? Accept Jesus Christ as your Savior before that final day arrives. We have nothing to lose except eternal salvation.

Would you not want that?

Illustration 29 - "Blow ye the trumpet in Zion and sound an alarm in My holy mountain: let all the inhabitants of the land tremble. "Joel 2 v1

BOOK 30 Amos

Context:

The Book of Amos takes place around 750-747 BC. Amos says he was not a prophet or a prophet's son but was a herdsman and gatherer of sycamore fruit. The Lord spoke to him as he followed the flock and said unto him, "Go, prophesy unto My people of Israel". Amos delivered God's messages to the northern kingdom and his words were not taken well. He was viewed just as a shepherd from the south and they put little worth in what he had to say. The northerners believed they were above this with their wealth and status, and they continued in their sinful ways. For them justice and bribery were their rule for legal outcomes. They had no love or mercy for the poor. They were in the pit of moral decay, and Amos continued to prophesy the outcome of God's judgement.

Application:

I ask myself, "Who am I but a teacher and architect? Who will listen to me? What impact will my words have?" I understand God's example of the plumb bob, being an architect. (Amos 7 v7-8). Its measure is always straight, and there is no questioning it. The same is true for God's plumb line for us which means we must align with its measure to be straight and upright in His sight.

Ask yourself, "Who am I? Where can I take Your message? Can I be God's instrument of change?" Are you ready to try? I will always remember what my grandfather told me as a young boy. He said, "Can't never could do anything." You can, and God knows you can make change. Don't wait! **Become an agent of change for God and others.**

Illustration 30 - "But I was a herdsman, and a gatherer of sycamore fruit." Amos 7 v14

BOOK 31 Obadiah
Context:

Obadiah has been identified as the prophet and author of this book. It was written most likely between 848 and 840 BC. This book is the shortest in the Old Testament with only 21 verses and takes about three minutes to read. This book is about God's condemnation of Edom for their sins against Israel and God. God's message is final. Edom will be destroyed completely. Even though the writings are short, the messages are clear.

Mistreatment of others may reap temporary victories, but it will eventually be repaid. Improper attitudes toward your brother will bring destruction.

Application:

These principals from Obadiah can be used everywhere, in the workplace, home, and with your friends. From the context we read, "As one sows, so shall he also reap", leading to another well-known statement, "Practice what you preach." Just be sure that what you practice does not lead to the mistreatment or the downfall of others.

Make sure that your pride does not prevent you from helping others. I am too good to lower myself to... You fill in the blank. The illustration on the right shows two needing help, and a prideful wealthy person seems bothered to help as though this is beneath him because of his false pride. Try to identify people around you, or your friends, who serve as examples humility and love. Fight oppression. Go and become a beacon not acting out of pride. Others will benefit and learn from you. God will overcome on our behalf. It's time we sow the garden of great actions, that when reaped, will be bountiful and purposeful for others.

OBADIAH

Illustration 31 - As One Sows, so will He also Reap

BOOK 32 Jonah
Context:

The book of Jonah was probably written in between 793 to 758 B.C. God asks Jonah to go to Nineveh and tell them of their immediate doom if they do not repent and return to God. Jonah goes in the opposite direction against God's will. He takes a ship to Tarshish. God becomes angry and in a storm on the journey the crew casts Jonah overboard. He is consumed by a large fish and repents while in the belly of the fish. God shows favor after three days and Jonah is cast alive on dry land. He finally travels to Nineveh and delivers the message of destruction in the coming days.

Everyone is alarmed, even the king! They all put on sack cloths, sit in ashes, and repent, and God is pleased. Jonah is upset and goes up on a hill to pout and watch the destruction of Nineveh in the blazing sun. God sprouts a leafy gourd to protect him and it dies the next day. Jonah is upset. God responds, "How can you be so concerned about this plant and not concerned of My compassion on people who are ignorant of right from wrong." God does save Nineveh. Later in the Bible you might also realize that it was also three days after Christ's death that He was resurrected!

Application:

Don't be a Jonah; disobedient, stubborn, someone who grumbles all the time. When asked to do a difficult task don't run in the other direction putting off the inevitable. Face your responsibilities head on with strength and confidence. Act in a positive and godly manner. Be fair and just. Deliver the message however hard it might seem. Who knows? Your response might lead to an opportunity that could **change someone's life** and their future in a very positive way.

Illustration 32- " And the LORD spake unto the fish, and it vomited out Jonah upon the dry land." Jonah 2 v10

BOOK 33 Micah
Context:

Micah was not identified as what we would call a mainstream prophet, a part of the establishment as we would know it. He was a man connected with the common agricultural people, and his messages directed to the government, relate to their needs and care. One of his most important messages was the forecasting of Christ. Micah 5 v2 "But thou, Bethlehem Ephratah, though thou be little among the thousands of Judah, yet out of thee shall He come forth unto me that is to be Ruler in Israel; Whose goings forth have been from of old, from everlasting." Micah talks about the judgement on Israel and the restoration of God's people. Micah was written in the 8th century B.C.

Application:

Two verses stand as life applications. First is Micah 6 v8 "O man, what is good; and what doth the LORD require of thee, but to do justly, and to love mercy, and to walk humbly with thy God?" The second is Micah 7 v8-9 "Rejoice not against me, O mine enemy: when I fall, I shall arise; when I sit in darkness, the LORD shall be a light unto me. I will bear the indignation of the LORD, because I have sinned against Him, until He plead my cause, and execute judgment for me: He will bring me forth to the light, and I shall behold His righteousness." When we have trouble in life, and we are in a dark place we know that God will have justice and love for us and will encourage us to move forward. If you are knocked down, get up! **Look for the light in your route as you move forward.** As it has been said about history, understand it, and try not to repeat its mistakes.

Illustration 33 - "When I sit in darkness the LORD shall be a light unto me...He will bring me forth to the light, and I shall behold His righteousness."" Micah 7 v 8-9

BOOK 34 Nahum
Context:

Scholars suggest that the book of Nahum was written about 615 B.C. Nineveh was saved from the judgement of God about 200 years earlier through the warnings of the prophet Jonah. The prophet Nahum again now tries to warn the king of impending destruction, which they ignore.

Nahum 2 v13 "Behold, I am against thee, saith the LORD of hosts, and I will burn her chariots in the smoke, and the sword shall devour thy young lions: and I will cut off thy prey from the earth, and the voice of thy messengers shall no more be heard."

Nahum 3 v3 "The horseman lifteth up both the bright sword and the glittering spear: and there is a multitude of slain, and a great number of carcasses; and there is no end of their corpses; they stumble upon their corpses."

Thus, Nineveh, once a great power, is now no more.

Application:

Just look around you. Do you know someone or a group that is on a destructive path? I know that if I was approached by a Christian who saw my route was leading to destruction and gave advice on how to avoid that destruction, **why would I not listen?**

Our life will pass by so quickly. We should be builders, not destroyers. If you see someone on a path of destruction offer them counsel, with humility and discernment. If bad times should come, be ready. If we fail, we must ask God to re-center us and redirect our purpose. You do not want to be like Nineveh!

NAHUM

Illustration 34 - Nineveh Is No More

BOOK 35 Habakkuk

Context:

This book took place around 630 or 629 B.C. While Habakkuk is identified as a prophet, he did not speak with kings, government officials, or the general people around him, like other prophets. His conversations were directly with God, questioning the justice and the reality of the Divine Providence. Habakkuk has two complaints. The first is:

Habakkuk 1 v13 "Your eyes are too pure to look on evil; You cannot tolerate wrongdoing. Why then do You tolerate the treacherous? Why are You silent while the wicked swallow up those more righteous than themselves?" Habakkuk just does not understand. God asks Habakkuk to write down His responses so that others may run when they read it. Woe to the greedy; Woe to him who covets evil gain; Woe to him who builds a town with bloodshed; Woe to him that causes you neighbor to be drunk for your advantage; Woe to him that is an Idolater of graven images. Habakkuk's lesson is that he had to live by faith because of everything happening around him and that he must understand that God works things out in His own way and in His own time.

Application:

Just turn on the TV or read the news; evil, injustice, and terrible influences are all around us. We must be like Habakkuk and be optimistic that God's plan is working and will be resolved in His timing. We can still cry out to God, and we can pray for intervention. Trust must be in Him. So, I say to you, life is not a bed of roses, but we can surely watch out for those thorns that can prick us in our life. Remember, there is a Glorious End and Beginning coming one day. **Avoid the thorns of life and help others, also.**

Illustration 35 - Habakkuk Crying out to God for Answers

BOOK 36 Zephaniah
Context:

Zephaniah is mentioned as the author in the beginning of the book. This writing is believed to have taken place around 640-609 B.C. Some believe that Zephaniah was a disciple of Isaiah because their themes are so similar. His heritage can be traced back to Hezekiah, confirming his lineage of prophets that served under one of the good kings (There were also bad kings in his lineage, as well). What stands out to me and gives me inspiration for the illustration is 1 v4 "I will also stretch out mine hand upon Judah, and upon all the inhabitants of Jerusalem; and I will cut off the remnant of Baal from this place, and the name of the Chemarims with the priests."

Find some time to read Zephaniah.

Application:

As you reflect on the previous pages in this book, you have read and discovered an overriding theme of destruction and redemption. Remember to practice what you preach. Others see your actions. God can see your actions and thoughts. I am not perfect. You are not perfect, but we can strive to make sure that the route in our life is Christ-centered. There are so many distractions around us and dramatic events. Sometimes it's hard to stay focused. We need to stay focused.

We need to walk the talk. If we fail, remember that God can restore us, and He can re-center us. God is serious about His relationship with us, and we need to be serious about our relationship with Him. **Time to get serious!**

ZEPHANIAH

Illustration 36 - God's Outstretched Hand is Over Us

BOOK 37 Haggai
Context:

The book of Haggai was written in 520 B.C. After the Jewish people returned from captivity in Babylon, they found that the temple in Jerusalem had been destroyed.

Haggai 1 v7 "Thus saith the LORD of hosts; Consider your ways. v8 Go up to the mountain, and bring wood, and build the house; and I will take pleasure in it, and I will be glorified, saith the LORD."

Application:

While this is one of the shortest books in the Old Testament, its impact is about the great rebuilding of the temple and rebuilding the church. In today's world this application has great emphasis. You don't have to go to the forest like Haggai (but in some parts of the world this still happens). Just think how God can empower you to rebuild His temple or church. As an architect, I have had the honor to design several church buildings. Some of these projects required rebuilding and some of them where totally new sanctuaries.

You don't have to be an architect to help rebuild your church or another's church. You can volunteer to help in the mission field to build or renovate a church. Your tithes can help with church building fund. You can build the church in other ways.

Invite friends to visit your church. That will help build up the church and bring others closer to God. You can teach classes or be on committees that will build the leadership and educational opportunities in your church. But never forget the power of prayer which helps sanctify, strengthen, and build up your church or synagogue.

HAGGAI

Illustration 37 - "Go up to the mountain, and bring wood, and build the house: and I will take pleasure in it, and I will be glorified, saith the Lord." Haggai 1 v8

BOOK 38 Zechariah
Context:

Zechariah, the prophet, lived during the reign of Darius around 520 B.C., who was governor over the district of Yehud Medinata. Some biblical scholars believe that several people wrote Zechariah. First, by Zechariah; second, by some of his disciples. The temple was being rebuilt during this period, also. This book includes the many visions or prophetic dreams (8), and historical messages of the Lord establishing His Kingdom over time. The verses that influenced my vision for the illustration from Zechariah are:

Zechariah 6 v1 "And I turned, and lifted up mine eyes, and looked, and, behold, there came four chariots out from between two mountains; and the mountains were mountains of brass. v2 in the first chariot were red horses; and in the second chariot black horses; v3 and in the third chariot white horses; and in the fourth chariot grisled and bay horses."

Read Zechariah and discover the other visions and messages.

Application:

Have you had dialogue lately with your pastor, minister, priest, or rabbi? Let me encourage you to speak with them and let me encourage you to encourage them. Let them know that their message is received and thank them for it. Go and tell others to come to your places of worship so that they can hear the truths of God. **If not you, then who?**

Illustration 38 - Zechariah's Dream

BOOK 39 Malachi

Context:

Yes, it is now the final chapter of the Old Testament. The Jews have now been in their homeland for more than 100 years after their captivity. Malachi means "messenger" in Hebrew. Malachi delivers many important messages on love, service, discipline, marriage, the Messiah, stewardship, faithfulness. He also delivers messages regarding the messenger coming, John the Baptist, who will prepare the way for Him. Also, Malachi delivers the message about Elijah appearing before the "great day of reckoning of the Lord" and preparing the way before Him. There are too many outstanding messages to fit into this context. Please find a Bible and read this last and important message from the Old Testament and next, enter the New Testament on our route.

Application:

Are we really any different today? The message is still valid, if we really want to be included in the Lamb's Book of Life. As a young boy, I remember taking the Scout Oath. Just think, if we substitute the word God for Scout "On my honor I will do my best to do my duty to God and my country, to obey God's Law, to help other people at all times, to keep myself physically strong, mentally awake and morally straight.' To do our best doesn't mean to just be a Sunday Christian!

Get in there and work it out. **Obey God's laws** (the Ten Commandments). If we are not spiritually strong, then how can we carry out God's mission for us? Be mentally awake so that you can discern right from wrong, good from evil, and be morally straight. Stay on the right route that will prepare you for an Everlasting Hereafter.

Illustration 39 - Malachi With the Priests Delivering God's Messages

LEAVING THE OLD TESTEMENT

ENTERING THE NEW TESTAMENT

BOOK 40 Matthew

Context:

The birth in Bethlehem; the wise men; the baptism and it's meanings; the many miracles performed; the blessed Scriptures; the multitudes that followed Christ; teaching His disciples: The first, Simon, who is called Peter, and Andrew, his brother; James, the son of Zebedee, and John his brother; Philip, and Bartholomew; Thomas and Matthew, the publican; James, the son of Alphaeus, and Lebbaeus, whose surname was Thaddaeus; Simon the Canaanite, and Judas Iscariot, who also betrayed Him. The confronting of the priests, His betrayal; the Lords supper, punishment, and final crucifixion; the resurrection after three days and Christ's appearing to many in Galilee, and much more! You must read this amazing book of the Bible!

Application:

What a truly remarkable book of the Bible! There are many applications, but to me the most important is that Jesus Christ gave us a powerful prayer to pray. If you have never prayed this prayer, find a quiet place where you can be alone and from your heart pray the prayer from Matthew 6 v9-13: "Our Father which art in heaven, Hallowed be Thy Name. Thy kingdom comes. Thy will be done in earth, as it is in heaven. Give us this day our daily bread. And forgive us our debts, as we forgive our debtors. And lead us not into temptation but deliver us from evil: For Thine is the kingdom, and the power, and the glory, forever. Amen"

Then in verse 14 He says, "For if ye forgive men their trespasses, your Heavenly Father will also forgive you." Do you truly want to be forgiven? **You must ask!**

MATTHEW

Illustration 40 - He Died to Save Us All from Sin. "Have we surely killed the Son of God?"

BOOK 41 Mark

Context:

Mark describes Christ's miracles, the journeys of Jesus, and His crucifixion. Amazing to read how Mark describes Christ's baptism, what happened to John the Baptist, the multitudes that followed Jesus wherever He went and how He fed them. Mark told of the many miracle healings: death then life; the blind that He made see; the crippled that He made walk; devils that were cast out, and many other miracles; the importance of children and their faith; and descriptions of how He dealt with the Pharisees.

What stood out to me was Mark 6 v56 "And whither so ever He entered, into villages, or cities, or country, they laid the sick in the streets, and besought Him that they might touch if it were but the border of His garment: and as many as touched Him were made whole."

Application:

My route through the book of Mark has left me with unmistakable values regarding faith and miracles. Has a miracle happened to you? Do you know someone that has experienced a miracle? What about the miracle of life? Miracles are only one part of God's wonders. Faith is another part.

Take some time before you continue your route to stop and pray now about your faith. If your faith is weak, pray that it will become stronger. If your faith is strong, pray that you might lead others to faith, for with faith, miracles can abound everywhere. **What better miracle could there be than to lead someone to Jesus Christ!** There are many examples of faith and miracles in the book of Mark. Read it to discover them for yourself.

Illustration 41 - They Laid the Sick in The Streets

BOOK 42 Luke
Context:

Luke, the physician, is writing to document meticulously the events of Christ which "emphasizes Jesus' love and care for those whom the Jewish leaders never even noticed.

1. Women
2. The poor
3. The socially, racially, and religiously ostracized
   a. Immoral women
   b. Samaritans
   c. Lepers
   d. Tax collectors
   e. Criminals
   f. Rebellious family members
   h. Gentiles[1]

Application:

It's amazing reading Luke and discovering the many types of people who were on the fringe that Jesus healed and forgave! Jesus did not have a clique! He was inclusive.

What would be your reaction if you stopped at an intersection where someone was begging, and they approached you, and offered to wash your feet? Oh no! What would you do? I can only imagine the level of humility and servanthood required of that person.

Let's try to be compassionate to others. If there are opportunities to help those in the categories listed in the context above let's reach out and minister to someone. It may lead them to ask forgiveness for their sins or life mistakes. **Ask yourself what would Jesus do?**

LUKE

Illustration 42 - She kissed His feet and anointed them with oil.

BOOK 43 John
Context:

The book of John was written around 85-95 A.D. There will also be I John, II John, III John, and the book of Revelation. In John, we read about his personal experiences with Jesus Christ and the life experiences as John encountered the teachings of Jesus, the miracles, the last supper, crucifixion, resurrection, and His reappearance.

Application:

There are so many possible applications from John to illustrate and use in an application. For me on this journey, the vision came to illustrate the Last Supper as this is in the last of the four gospels (Matthew, Mark, Luke, and John). Christ has clearly described to His disciples, and to us, the route for eternal salvation. As it is said in John 3 v16 "For God so loved the world, that He gave His only begotten Son, that whosoever believeth in Him should not perish, but have everlasting life". John 4 v14 "But whosoever drinketh of the water that I shall give him shall never thirst; but the water that I shall give him shall be in him a well of water springing up into everlasting life."

Have you shared the Gospel with anyone? What are you waiting for? Life is short. Who can you lead to salvation? If you haven't accepted Christ, it is as simple as ABC: Admit that you are a sinner and ask for God's forgiveness. B: Believe in Jesus and become a child of God by receiving Christ. C: Confess that Jesus is your Lord and commit your life to Him. As in the Last Supper, Christ has prepared his disciples and his followers to go out and share the Gospel. Are you finding your route in life? What will be your next decision? **Its as simple as ABC**.

JOHN

Illustration 43 - "The Last Supper" Christ's Last Instructions to His Disciples

BOOK 44 Acts
Context:

Luke wrote the book of Acts to Theophilus around 80-90 A.D. Luke chronicles the establishment of the Church in Jerusalem, then how the church expands to Judea and Samaria and then to the ends of the earth. Luke continues to explain the acceptance of the Gentiles in the faith and the problems of convincing priests that God is not just a God for them but for everyone. These times were tough, as Stephen was stoned to death, and Paul was imprisoned by the Romans. The disciples spread the Gospel everywhere, baptizing and appointing other disciples to spread the Word and grow the Christian faith.

Application:

Don't let life imprison you! Break the chains that bind you. Thank God for all the blessings and opportunities He provides you. Be of good spirit. Paul was imprisoned for two years and still was able to spread the message of Jesus Christ to the world (The Romans, the Jews, the Greeks, and other peoples of the world).

Ask yourself," What is preventing me from sharing the Gospel?" Free yourself from those barriers that are holding you back and help change God's world in the name of Jesus Christ. You can do it through your business, community service, one on one with someone, in your family, in your church, by mission outreach, and also in tragic situations. In ancient times this outreach of the Gospel started in Jerusalem, went to Judea. And now to the ends of the earth!

Start in your church and city, or find another region in your country, or even go the ends of the earth. **Everywhere is waiting for you!**

Illustration 44 - Paul Sharing the Gospel While Under House Arrest in Rome

BOOK 45 Romans
Context:

While in the Greek city of Corinth around 57 A.D., Paul wrote a letter to the Church in Rome to strengthen the basic Christian doctrine there. Persecution had not yet begun there but would soon start under the rule of a young King Nero. While in the seaport of Corinth, there was a huge diversity of people's cultures and prolific immoral practices. Paul saw the immoralities taking place about him and wrote about them. In Romans 12 Paul talks about us as a living sacrifice and what God's plan is for our lives. He continues to write that when we love one another, our spiritual gifts emerge, and he continues to explain the principles of Christian life in Romans 12 v9-21.

All the writings in Romans lead to a gateway of Christian living and salvation. Paul acknowledges that he hopes to see the believers after his trip to Spain. Little does he know what lies ahead!

Application:

In this age of technology, how many of us still write? We can take a lesson from Paul and write as well. Write someone to share your faith. It can take many forms. It might be a book as I am writing, perhaps a song or poem. You could write your children to share your faith, you could write a leaflet about Christianity, and leave it somewhere that a stranger might encounter it. Read Romans as an example from Paul's letter. Writing is a great way to share the value and faith in Christianity. Pick up a pencil or get on the keyboard and share your heart and Christian values with others. You are only one word away from starting! **What will your first writing say?**

ROMANS

Illustration 45 - Paul Writing to the Roman Church from Corinth while in Greece

BOOK 46 I Corinthians
Context:

On Paul's third mission trip, he went to Ephesus for three years. While in Ephesus he received news from the household of Chloe that there was a rift in the church in Corinth that was threatening its life and ministry (dissolution, idolatry and theological confusion). The church asked Paul for guidance and clarification. Paul wrote them a letter to remind them of the doctrine of the Christian Church.

Paul's letter tries to address the areas of weaknesses and immorality, to set straight the way of correct teaching, to reinforce the meaning and purpose of the Lord's Supper, and to correct misinformation concerning the resurrection. Paul instructs Timotheus to deliver his letter and message.

Read I Corinthians. "For we are one body in Christ."

Application:

Oh, the seeds of the devil seem to want to sprout everywhere and the Church is not immune. Have you observed discord in your church? Were you the seed of discord? If we want God's garden to prosper, we must be of the right spirit and of one accord. We must love one another, we must share and spread the same spirit and beliefs that were in Paul's letters. This is what Christ wants for us.

I know this is a different time and place, but the principles remain the same. My application is to practice what Christ has preached. **Love one another and go out and share the Gospel.** May the grace of our Lord Jesus Christ be with you, and my love be with you all in Christ Jesus. Amen.

I CORINTHIANS

Illustration 46 - Timotheus Reading the Letter of Encouragement to the Church in Corinth From the Apostle Paul

BOOK 47 II Corinthians
Context:

Paul wrote a second letter to the Corinthians as they continued to struggle in their beliefs. Paul reminded the church of the importance of tithing and the importance of supporting the mission of saints in the field. Paul also shared about his sufferings. II Corinthians 11 v6-7 (find a Bible and read this account). He reminds us to "Walk by faith, not sight." He reminded the Church in Corinth to remember the brutal treatment he received, but by the grace of God and Jesus Christ, that faith sustained him. The letter he wrote to Corinth should suspend the question of his integrity and remind the Church of the route in life they should take.

Application:

"For we walk by faith, not sight" while choosing to stay on the right route. Can you imagine having so much faith and joy that you would jump out of a boat to walk on water to greet Jesus? Peter did. But he was distracted by the sounds of the wind and sank into the waters and cried out "Lord Save me!" Ask yourself these questions.

Do you let your Christian faith slip in the workplace? Do you support someone face to face, but talk about them behind their backs? Do you hide things you have done to protect your job? Do you see what others are doing and copy them, knowing it is wrong? Transparency is important. Are you the same yesterday, today, and will be tomorrow? Are you applying these principles in your life and church as well? Remember to keep your eyes on Jesus, keep your faith growing strong, and stay on the right route in your life. This is hard for all of us, yes? But we can do it when we **let the Holy Spirit guide and empower us!**

II CORINTHIANS

Illustration 47- "Oh Peter, you of little faith." Matthew 14 v31

BOOK 48 Galatians
Context:

What really spoke to me from Galatians were these verses: 5 v1 "Stand fast therefore in the liberty where with Christ hath made us free, and be not entangled again with the yoke of bondage." v19 "Now the works of the flesh are manifest, which are these; Adultery, fornication, uncleanness, lasciviousness, v20 Idolatry, witchcraft, hatred, variance, emulations, wrath, strife, seditions, heresies, v21 Envyings, murders, drunkenness, revellings, and such like: of the which I tell you before, as I have also told you in time past, that they which do such things shall not inherit the kingdom of God. v22 But the fruit of the Spirit is love, joy, peace, longsuffering, gentleness, goodness, faith, v23 Meekness, temperance: against such there is no law. v24 And they that are Christ's have crucified the flesh with the affections and lusts. v25 If we live in the Spirit, let us also walk in the Spirit. v26 Let us not be desirous of vain glory, provoking one another, envying one another."

Application:

The choices are clear in Galatians; follow the route of sin or follow the route of Christ. There are many songs about the chains of sin being broken and being set free, or about laying our troubles and sins down before Him. My applications this time are a little different. Find these songs on YouTube and **listen** to them: Chris Tomlin – "Resurrection Power"; Matt Maher – "What a Friend"; Ben Glover, David Crowder, Matt Maher – "Come as You Are".

I have found that music can be spiritually moving. I pray that these songs will also move you spiritually, as they have done so to me!

Illustration 48 - Lay Down your Burdens, Lay Down your Sins, and Let your Chains be Broken

BOOK 49 Ephesians
Context:

While Paul was still in prison in Rome around 62 A.D., he wrote to the Ephesians. His letter was to clarify the old law under Abraham versus the new law (principles) of Jesus Christ. This book has much content that I remember hearing when I was a young boy. One is Paul's description of the "armor of God" in Ephesians 6 v13-18.

Ephesians is a must read! Read, don't wait. Find a Bible! What are you waiting for?

Application:

1.Belt of truth: Try to be truthful in both your heart and mind daily. Seek the Lord's truth by reading His Word the Bible.

2.Breastplate of Righteousness: Create a righteous Christian lifestyle that you can put into practice as those actions can protect us from temptation and sin.

3: Shoes: They are your foundation and can take you places anywhere to continue to spread His Word.

4: Shield of Faith: Just as it implies, your faith can protect you from many uncertainties and challenges. Don't lose faith.

5: Helmet of Salvation: It's your mind. Always remember Christ's Salvation and teachings.

6: Sword of the Spirit: It's His Word (the Bible). Truth always wins.

Put on the full armor of God!

EPHESIANS

Illustration 49 - "Wherefore, take unto you the Whole Armor of God." Ephesians 6 v13

BOOK 50 Philippians
Context:

While Paul was still in prison in Rome around 60-62 A.D., he wrote also to the Philippians while there were still some crises in the churches. Paul wanted to thank them and to tell them of his appreciation for them (because of their financial support among other things). In his letter, he describes how they should continue to advance the Gospel and reminds them of the importance of an intimate relationship in Christ.

Paul continues to encourage them to press on even if there is turmoil, and to rejoice in the Lord. Philippians 2 v29 "For unto you it is given in the behalf of Christ, not only to believe on Him, but also to suffer for His sake". And to live as Christians and to have servants' hearts and humility just as Jesus Christ displayed." Philippians 2 v14-15 "Do all things without murmurings and disputings. That ye may be blameless and harmless, the sons of God, without rebuke, in the midst of a crooked and perverse nation, among whom ye shine as lights in the world."

Application:

As a child, I remember the prayer my mother taught me to say every night. "Now I lay me down to sleep. I pray the Lord to my soul to keep. If I should die before I wake, I pray the Lord my soul to take."

We are never too young or too old to pray. Prayer should be a part of our daily life. If you have not prayed today, then pray before the sun sets. He is always there waiting to hear from you. The communication can start with each of us. Through prayer we can become beacons to others. **Let us shine as lights in the World**.

PHILIPPIANS

Illustration 50 - "Be careful about nothing; but in everything by prayer and supplication with thanksgiving let your requests be made known unto God." Philippians 4 v6

BOOK 51 Colossians
Context:

Paul continues to be imprisoned in Rome around 60-62 A.D. As you have discerned by now, Paul is writing many of the churches to encourage and help them stay on the correct path in Christ. In his letters, Paul continues to remind followers to be wary of unorthodox teachings from those who have penetrated the churches in Colossae. He sends Tychicus and Onesimus to deliver his messages to believers, and to apply those to their teachings.

Application:

It seems that attacks can come from everywhere.

Paul's message rings loud and clear to the Colossians and myself (It's as though the message was sent to me). Colossians 1 v9 "For this cause we also, since the day we heard it, do not cease to pray for you, and to desire that ye might be filled with the knowledge of His will in all wisdom and spiritual understanding. v10 That ye might walk worthy of the Lord unto all pleasing, being fruitful in every good work, and increasing in the knowledge of God."

As I awake in the morning, my prayers include giving thanks for God's blessings and opportunities. Pray that you will grow spiritually and that He will provide you with what your need to "be fruitful in every good work" as you serve others. Pray and ask. **How I can increase my knowledge of you, God, and how can I apply that knowledge to spread Your Word?** It's wonderful knowing that someone is praying for me. There is always someone ready to pray for you. Just let that need be known because we don't have to walk this path alone!

114

COLOSSIANS

Illustration 51 - Here the Colossians greet Tychicus. We should know that we are never alone when we are doing Christ's work. He is always by our side.

BOOK 52 I Thessalonians
Context:

Paul was concerned about the church in Thessalonica. After he left and went to Corinth, he sent Timothy to observe the situation there. When Timothy returned, he had good news. Despite the persecution of Christians, the church remained strong and was an example for others.

Their concern was that those they loved in Christ and died would not miss out on the Second coming of the Lord. Paul's response was: I Thessalonians 4 v15 "For this we say unto you by the Word of the Lord, that we which are alive and remain unto the coming of the Lord shall not prevent them which are asleep. v16 For the Lord Himself shall descend from heaven with a shout, with the voice of the archangel, and with the trump of God: and the dead in Christ shall rise first: v17 Then we which are alive and remain shall be caught up together with them in the clouds, to meet the Lord in the air: and so shall we ever be with the Lord."

Application:

Take some time to resuscitate your faith and show your love to others. Make it a point to read your Bible this week. Spend time and evaluate your own walk with God. Talk with a non-Christian about your faith. You can visit someone in the hospital. Help a friend or neighbor with work (your elderly neighbor might need the grass cut). Go shopping for someone. **Take your role seriously as a Christian, plant seeds, and build bridges for Christ!**

Illustration 52 - "For the Lord Himself shall descend from heaven with a shout... and with the trump of God: and the dead in Christ shall rise first." I Thessalonians 4 v16

BOOK 53 II Thessalonians
Context:

In his overview of II Thessalonians, Chuck Swindoll indicates that it was within months that Paul wrote the second letter to them. Paul reminds them of the trouble coming to those that persecute them and that they will get their due in the end. II Thessalonians Chapter 1 v5-9: v5 "Which is a manifest token of the righteous judgment of God, that ye may be counted worthy of the kingdom of God, for which ye also suffer. v6 Seeing it is a righteous thing with God to recompense tribulation to them that trouble you; v7 And to you who are troubled rest with us, when the Lord Jesus shall be revealed from heaven with His mighty angels, v8 In flaming fire taking vengeance on them that know not God and that obey not the Gospel of our Lord Jesus Christ: v9 Who shall be punished with everlasting destruction from the presence of the Lord, and from the glory of His power."

Application:

Paul reminds us not to be busybodies. So, don't butt into situations that are not your business, nor should we be lazy in work and our faith. II Thessalonians 3 v10 "For even when we were with you, this we commanded you, that if any would not work, neither should he eat." As difficult as this sounds, also try not to be in debt. **Pray that God would count you worthy of His calling when the time comes.**

Will you be in the flames or in glory when the end time comes? The decision is yours. If you need help, seek out a Christian or begin by finding a Bible and start reading the New Testament.

II THESSALONIANS

Illustration 53 - The Angel in Flaming Fire Taking Vengeance on Them That Know not God

BOOK 54 I Timothy
Context:

Many suggest that Paul wrote to Timothy after his release from prison around 63 A.D. Paul had met Timothy more than ten years earlier, became his mentor, calls him his son in Christ, and sends him on many outreach mission engagements with other churches. In 1 Timothy, Paul, as his mentor, reminds him how unworthy he himself is. Timothy 1 v11-13 "…his unfaithfulness and ignorance in unbelief. Then the grace of Christ fell upon him to become a teacher in the ministry (see illustration 54 - Saul/Paul's encounter with Christ on the road to Damascus where Paul's life was changed by Jesus Christ after His resurrection). Paul reminds Timothy to stay strong and describes the leadership qualities necessary for work in the ministry, and the role of women in the church, and to let no one despise his youth, to but be an example of believers in word, conversation, charity, spirit, faith, and in purity. He reminds Timothy to flee earthly things which are the root of all evil and to "fight the good fight of faith, lay hold on eternal life, whereunto thou art also called, and hast professed a good profession before many witnesses." 1 Timothy 6 v12.

Application:

When I think of the students I have taught and people I have led in business, I pray that they will remember me as a good mentor that had special values (Christ based). I have tried to not let my Christian values be compromised with those I have led. If you need to freshen your values, read I Timothy.

You can be a mentor of Christian values to others. Be the right kind of leader. **You can change a life. Start now!**

I TIMOTHY

Illustration 54 - "And I thank Christ Jesus our Lord, who hath enabled me, for that He counted me faithful, putting me into the ministry." I Timothy v12

BOOK 55 II Timothy
Context:

As mentor to Timothy, Saint Paul writes his final letter to his spiritual son. We should be reminded of the tremendous faith that Paul had and kept throughout all the pain and suffering, beatings, shipwrecks, and imprisonment. Paul realizes that his time is near an end as he writes:

2 Timothy 4 v6 "For I am now ready to be offered, and the time of my departure is at hand. v7 I have fought a good fight, I have finished my course, I have kept the faith. v8 Henceforth there is laid up for me a crown of righteousness, which the Lord, the Righteous Judge, shall give me at that day: and not to me only, but unto all them also that love His appearing." Paul later dies in Rome around the age of 62.

Application:

Is there someone in your life who has been a rock of your foundation? It could be a parent, a sibling, spouse, coach, pastor, co-worker or teacher. For me, one was my high school basketball coach, Don Handcock. Don and his wife mentored me when there was an absence of a father in my life. The other is my wife who came into my life when I had wandered off my route. Her love and joy are overflowing and filled me with what was missing in my life. I tell everyone that she is the angel that God sent to me. I must now thank others that have solidified my foundation in my Christian faith and life as I continue to grow.

Whoever your mentors were or are, seek them out, if possible, and thank them for their Godly influence in your life. As we approach the end of our days will Christ say you fought the good fight, stayed the course, and were a rock in the foundation of others?

122

Illustration 55 - Paul Writing his Last Letter to Timothy

BOOK 56 Titus
Context:

Titus became the truth keeper and spreader of correct Christian doctrine. Examples: God's grace saves us from our sins; God instructs us to live boldly and upright, with love for our neighbors; to help those that need help; and to live lives in Christ's power. Paul specifically instructs Titus: Titus 1 v5-9 v5 "For this cause left I thee in Crete, that thou shouldest set in order the things that are wanting, and ordain elders in every city, as I had appointed thee. v6 If any be blameless, the husband of one wife, having faithful children not accused of riot or unruly. v7 For a bishop must be blameless, as the steward of God; not self-willed, not soon angry, not given to wine, no striker, not given to filthy lucre; v8 but a lover of hospitality, a lover of good men, sober, just, holy, temperate; v9 holding fast the faithful Word as he hath been taught, that he may be able by sound doctrine both to exhort and to convince the gainsayers."

Application:

Paul's message to Titus is about self-giving love through the grace of Jesus Christ, having His compassion. It is that compassion and love we need to have for others.

My application is to ask Jesus into your heart, if He is not there now. If He is in your heart, then I would ask you to pray "Lord, what can I do for You?" Listen and look for God. He will open a door for you to walk through so you can take your heart and your gifts to others. Yes, and even take others lovingly by the hand and help to lead them through God's door to serve others everywhere. **What will be your mission?**

TITUS

Illustration 56 - Titus Ordaining Elders in the Christian church on the Greek Island of Crete

BOOK 57 Philemon
Context:

Philemon, who was a slaveowner, was called a fellow worker. He worked closely with Paul. When Paul became a prisoner in Rome, Onesimus, a slave of Philemon, stole from his master and fled to Rome. When Onesimus was in Rome, he crossed paths with Paul and because of their earlier connection, Onesimus stayed and helped Paul and became a Christian convert. When Paul became aware of what was done, he later sends Onesimus back to Philemon in Colossae with a letter and asks Philemon to forgive Onesimus, to take him back as a partner in Christ, and whatever his debt was, Paul agreed to pay it. Philemon 1 v17 "If thou count me therefore a partner, receive him as myself. v18 If he hath wronged thee, or oweth thee ought, put that on mine account."

Paul wanted Philemon to accept his slave Onesimus back as a brother in Christ, forgive him, and send him back to Paul to help him in God's service.

Application:

This was a short book with a huge message. Have you ever forgiven someone their debt? My wife and I have had loved ones steal from us. We have repaid the debt of loved ones. I don't say this to be pompous. It was a really difficult thing to do, but God always seems to provide for us. I still love them and hope that our example one day will be put in to practice by them. My question is, could you forgive someone's debt? Could you welcome someone back that has wronged you? Christ forgave our sins. Can you forgive someone else's sins? **Forgive someone today.**

PHILEMON

Illustration 57 - Onesimus Returns to Philemon with a Letter from Paul (The thief returns to the scene, born again!)

BOOK 58 Hebrews
Context:

The book was probably written sometime in the mid to late 60 A.D. The author describes the First Covenant, the law of Moses for the Hebrews, the importance of the ritual of blood sacrifice, the cleansing for our sins, and the roles of the priests. Then there is the description of the second Covenant when God sent us His Son Jesus Christ, who was sinless and became the Lamb who shed His blood for us as sacrifice to forgive all the sins of the world. Now that is our covenant for life for all Jews and Gentiles alike. Hebrews 6 v 17-19 v17 "Wherein God, willing more abundantly to show unto the heirs of promise the immutability of his counsel, confirmed it by an oath. v18 That by two immutable things, in which it was impossible for God to lie, we might have a strong consolation, who have fled for refuge to lay hold upon the hope set before us. v19 Which hope we have as an anchor of the soul, both sure and steadfast, and which entered into that within the veil."

Application:

We do not have to see to have faith as told in Hebrews. Hope is the anchor of our soul. Make sure your anchor is adequate, and it will keep you sure and steadfast. Make sure your faith will let you give thanks to God, and that your faith will encourage your good works and sharing.

Jesus Christ, the same yesterday, and today, and forever! **Set your anchor today in faith and be prepared to take it with you as you continue your route in life.** That anchor of faith will keep you from drifting into troubled storms in life.

HEBREWS

Illustration 58 - We do not have to see. Hope is the anchor of our soul.

BOOK 59 James

Context:

The author of the book of James is thought to be the half-brother of Jesus. James was later referred to as the pillar of the Church. For James, faith must produce change in one life or it's worthless. It is noted that James was not a believer until after Christ's resurrection and, oh, how that changed his belief and his life, and others through his words and actions!

Application

Olin Hudson applications of James (paraphrased):

1.**Be Swift to Hear:** "Let every man be swift to hear, slow to speak, slow to wrath." If we are not swift to hear what God has to say, then we will not be able to live the way He wants us to live.

2.**Lay Aside All Filthiness:** In application of God's Word, we must take ourselves down from the throne of our lives and lay aside our evil practices.

3.**Receive God's Word in Meekness:** Once we have taken ourselves off the throne of our lives then we need to put God in that position. When we meekly receive His Word, we are saying that we will submit our will to His. His Word is what will rule our lives.

4.**Be Doers of the Word:** Application of anything is much more difficult than the mere knowledge of that thing. The same difficulty is present when discussing the application of God's Word in our lives. James has given us guidelines, so that we can become "effectual doers" of God's Word. Put these steps into practice and stop deceiving yourselves!

Read James in the Bible. It will only take a short time!

JAMES

Illustration 59 – "Submit yourselves therefore to God. Resist the devil, and he will flee from you." James 4 v7

BOOK 60 I Peter
Context:

Around 64 A.D. Christians in Asia Minor where under persecution, and Peter wrote to them (both Jews and Gentiles). Peter pointed out the importance of being strong in their faith and says it well in I Peter 2 v9 "But ye are a chosen generation, a royal priesthood, an holy nation, a peculiar people; that ye should shew forth the praises of Him Who hath called you out of darkness into His marvelous light." Peter also encouraged them to act and live as Jesus did. I Peter 3 v14 "but even if you suffer for doing what is right, God will reward you for it. So, don't worry or be afraid of their threats. v15 Instead, you must worship Christ as Lord of your life. And if someone asks about your hope as a believer, always be ready to explain it." v17 "Remember, it is better to suffer for doing good, if that is what God wants, than to suffer for doing wrong! v18 Christ suffered for our sins once for all time." He never sinned, but He died for sinners to bring you safely home to God. He suffered physical death, but He was raised to life in the Spirit.

Application

We all go through trials, tribulations, and suffering. Your faith will give you the strength to push through those trials as they are temporary. In the darkness of those times, move to that Christian light in you and to Him who shines brightest. Christ will lead you through and back on the correct route in your life. So now I ask you to stop and take a moment think about what your life has been. Next, think about where your life can be if your "Route in Life" follows Christ's principles. **Is today a new day in your life?**

I PETER

Illustration 60 - " Show forth the praises of Him Who hath called you out of darkness into His marvelous light."
I Peter 2 v9

BOOK 61 II Peter
Context:

Peter writes a second letter to the Christians in Asia Minor about 65-68 A.D. as they continue to suffer from persecutions and false teachings. Knowing that his life is soon at its end (later Peter is crucified), he wants to remind the Church to beware of false teachers. He reminds them of some guiding principles which include faith, virtue, knowledge, temperance, patience, godliness, brotherly kindness; and charity. If these things are within, you will not stumble nor will you be unfruitful in the knowledge and practice of the Lord Jesus Christ.

Application

As an academician for almost forty years, knowledge is the king. We have to know to instruct others. We want that knowledge to be truthful, and the image that came to my mind for this book is when Peter describes his meeting the reincarnate Christ on the Mount. 2 Peter 1 v18 "And this Voice which came from heaven we heard, when we were with Him in the holy mount." Verification of knowledge gets no better than that because Peter was also there with James and John.

My application: Find a New Testament and read Christ's own Words. If you are not in a church, find one that preaches the True Gospel (not an I'm ok, you're ok, worldly church). What can be better than having eternal salvation and sharing your Christ-like love with family, friends, community, nation, and the world. **What can be better than sharing Christ?**

II PETER

Illustration 61 - "And this Voice which came from heaven we heard, when we were with Him in the holy mount." 2 Peter 1 v18

BOOK 62 I John

Context:

John writes this letter to churches in the region of Ephesus about 90 A.D., to churches he had probably ministered to in his earlier missions and church plantings. It is suggested that these writings came from Patmos while he was in exile there. John talks about the light and darkness in faith. 1 John 1 v4-7 v4 "And these things write we unto you, that your joy may be full. v5 This then is the message which we have heard of Him, and declare unto you, that God is Light, and in Him is no darkness at all. v6 If we say that we have fellowship with Him, and walk in darkness, we lie, and do not live by the truth. v7 but if we walk in the light, as he is in the light, we have fellowship one with another, and the blood of Jesus Christ his Son cleanseth us from all sin."

John talks about right versus wrong, light versus dark-ness, and love of God versus love of the world. John also speaks about love in action. I John 3 v18 "My little children, let us not love in word, neither in tongue; but in deed and in truth."

Application

What a perfect book for now because of today's world. It seems people are persecuted just for not agreeing with the position of another person, especially about a political position or a view about life itself. There is truly light and darkness in our times, there is truly good and evil in our times. The choice is ours to be the seeds of light, the seeds of love, the seeds of truth, the seeds of faith, and the seeds of action in the name of God and Jesus Christ. We can help others to move from the darkness into the Light. **Will you be a leader for Christ?** There are many people that need you!

Illustration 62 - " Beloved, let us love one another: for love is of God; and everyone that loveth is born of God, and knoweth God." I John 4 v7

BOOK 63 II John
Context:

John addresses the letter to "the chosen lady and her children". It is thought this letter was written around 90 A.D. while John was in exile on the island of Patmos. It is further thought that this letter could have been written to a woman and her children that he knew while he was in the mission field, or it could have a metaphorical meaning "the lady" (being the church) and "the children" (the Christians of the church). This is the shortest book in the New Testament with only 13 verses. In those few verses much is said about love, truth, obedience, and false teachers.

Application

What stood out to me was 2nd John v4. "I rejoiced greatly that I found of thy children walking in truth, as we have received a commandment from the Father."

As parents we lead, pray, and encourage our children to walk in faith, truth, and love. Later in 2nd John it mentions in v10 "If there come any unto you, and bring not this doctrine, receive him not into your house, neither bid him God speed." Do we send away the bad and evil that could influence our children until such time that they can mature and stand alone on their faith?

My illustration is of the woman and her children whom she has nurtured to walk in faith. We need to be strong for our children and family in Christ. In the Church we all are brothers and sisters and our pastor or priest can help us to walk in truth, love, faith, and obedience, and to be on the lookout for false teachings. **Will you help to mentor your brothers and sisters in Christ, and your children?**

II JOHN

Illustration 63 - "I rejoiced greatly that I found of thy children walking in Truth, as we have received a Commandment from the Father." 2 John 1 v4

BOOK 64 III John
Context:

This is the last epistle John wrote while still in exile on the island of Patmos. John is nearing the end of his life and he is the only disciple not to be martyred. It is suspected that this epistle was written around 90 A.D. John writes to Gaius, who was a leader of one of the Asia Minor Churches. Diotrephes, an elder in another church, is not willing to receive them (read 3rd John v9-10 to understand his complaint). John then writes and commends the works of Gaius, sharing that he is true to the Word, and that his church continues to welcome ministers, which is good news! It seems that Diotrephes continues to refuse traveling missionaries and ministers of the Gospel.

Application

Churches should openly welcome other ministers, priests, and missionaries, as they bring and share with others the Good News of Jesus Christ in brotherly love. If you have not supported your church's mission work or outreach, consider doing so. Are you ready for a life changing experience?

Have you considered community mission outreach, global mission participation, or opening your home to receive missionary guests for short stays while they communicate with your church congregation?

Consider praying for missionaries abroad that minister to others. Most of all, consider a life changing experience by receiving Jesus Christ into your heart. The rest will fall into place. Mission work will change your life. **Are you ready to have your life changed?**

III JOHN

Illustration 64 - Gaius and his Church Receive and Welcome a Minister from Abroad

BOOK 65 Jude
Context:

The book is most likely written by Jude, the brother of James, Joses, Simon, and Jesus Christ. Some think that these were full siblings, half-brothers, or cousins of Christ. Jude really didn't become a true follower of Christ until after the crucifixion and resurrection. Jude traveled to many cities spreading the Word and his powerful faith in Christ. Jude's letter is to warn of false teachers in the Church and also warning of past Biblical consequences.

Jude indicates that false teachers need to be detached from the church and condemned. Jude indicates that we should build each other up in faith and truth. Jude 1 v20-21 v20 "But ye, beloved, building up yourselves on your most holy faith, praying in the Holy Ghost, v21 Keep yourselves in the love of God, looking for the mercy of our Lord Jesus Christ unto eternal life."

Application

In today's world there is much false teaching taking place in churches, in education, and in politics. Many are not speaking the truth but rather building themselves up for their own gratifications. As Christians, we must stand up for truth and be strong in our faith.

Read into my illustration what you will. Are they speaking the Truth, or do they speak evil? My application for you is to **always be in search of Truth and listen carefully to what others say.** Be sure you are satisfied that the truth is being communicated. Love one another and be truthful and faithful in all that you do.

JUDE

Illustration 65 - "But these speak evil of those things which they know not: but what they know naturally, as brute beasts, in those things they corrupt themselves." Jude 1 v10

BOOK 66 Revelation
Context:

We know that while John was in exile on the island of Patmos, he was put there because of his activities as a Christian missionary. The book of Revelation was written in John's later years, around 95 A.D. Revelation comes from the Greek word "apocalypse". Apocalypse means the telling or sharing of something unknown or yet to come. John begins to explain the beginning of a series of events.

Revelation 1 v10-20 v10 "I was in the Spirit on the Lord's day, and heard behind me a Great Voice, as of a trumpet, v11 Saying, I am Alpha and Omega, the First and the Last: and, What thou seest, write in a book, and send it unto the seven churches which are in Asia; unto Ephesus, and unto Smyrna, and unto Pergamos, and unto Thyatira, and unto Sardis, and unto Philadelphia, and unto Laodicea. v12 And I turned to see the Voice that spake with me. And being turned, I saw seven golden candlesticks; v13 And in the midst of the seven candlesticks One like unto the Son of Man, clothed with a garment down to the foot, and girt about the paps with a golden girdle. v14 His head and His hairs were white like wool, as white as snow; and His eyes were as a flame of fire; v15 And His feet like unto fine brass, as if they burned in a furnace; and His voice as the sound of many waters. v16 And He had in His right hand seven stars: and out of His mouth went a sharp two-edged sword: and His countenance was as the sun shineth in his strength. v17 and when I saw Him, I fell at his feet as dead. And He laid His right hand upon me, saying unto me, Fear not; I am the First and the Last: v18 I am He that liveth, and was dead; and, behold, I am alive for evermore, Amen; and have the keys of hell and of death. v19 Write the things which thou hast seen, and the things which are, and the things which shall be hereafter; v20 the mystery of the seven stars which thou sawest in My right hand, and the seven golden candlesticks. The seven stars are the angels of the seven churches: and the seven candlesticks which thou sawest are the seven churches."

Application

Wow! Wow! And Wow! What a journey this has been for me, and I hope also for you. We started at the beginning of the Bible and traveled to the end of the Bible, and now we are waiting for the New Beginning. I hope that the previous 65 applications will be helpful for your route in your life.

If you have wandered onto a different route, I pray that this book and the Bible will get you back on the right route in your life. If you are on the right route in your life, I pray that these writings will enable you to see and experience life in a way you have never done before. I pray that this route will take you to encounters with others who have gone astray, and that you can give them guidance that will help them to decide on positive outcomes that might lead them to Christ and change their earthly and eternal life!

My application for you is to share your faith with your spouse, your family, your friends, your church, your business, and your community, and wherever life takes you. My prayer is for you to be strong in your faith. What do you have to lose? Revelation is an incredible accounting of what is to come, and speaking for myself, I can only imagine what it will be like! Perhaps one day we will meet here or There, and we can share our incredible routes in life!

146

REVELATION

Acknowledgements
Credits:

I would like to thank the following people for giving me permission to use the likeness of their image in this book. Some were my students and colleagues, but many were total strangers. Sometimes within my community and in my travels, I would be led to go up to a stranger. I would share with them that they had a certain Biblical nature about them. I would ask if I could photograph them and use their image in my book.

Thanks again to all of you:

Judges: Kevin Smith; John Kelly; Haley Moore; Hap Burn; Herbie Burns; David Koonce; Chris Stowe; Brent Cook

Samuel: David Burns

I Chronicles: John Moormann

Nehemiah: Pavlo Haran

Daniel: Richard Johnson;

Amos: Josh Guiton

Jonah: Richard Patterson Zephaniah: Jerry Pegram

Haggai: Charles Blackburn

Matthew: Bill Beardlser; Hap Burn; Haley Moore; Moil Nekp

Joshua: M Logan; Lamar Conner; Richard Laytona

Mark: Nickolas Mabe; Josh Guiton; Michael Wheeler

Luke: Nickolas Mabe

John: Joshua M Logan; Anthony Hobbs; Kevin Smith; Moll S. Nekp; Richard Layton; Larry Braden; John J. Eakins; Nickolas Mabe

Acts & Romans: Moll S. Nekp

2nd Corinthians: Michael Wheeler; Nickolas Mabe

Philippians: Moll S. Nekp
Colossians: Jerry Pegram
1st Timothy: Moll S. Nekp
2nd Timothy: Moll S. Nekp
Titus: Tony Durham
2nd John: Kevin Smith; John Kelly; Tony Durham
3rd John: Nickolas Mabe: Brandon Throckmorton
Revelation: Anthony Hobbs

Footnotes:

1.Luke the Historian: The Gospel of Luke, Bible Lessons International, 112 N. Columbus St., Marshall, Texas 75670, https://bible.org/book/export/html/21296 , (July 25, 2018)

2.Charles R. Swindoll, "Hebrews", The Bible Teaching Ministry of Charles R. Swindoll, Post Office Box 5000, Frisco, Texas, 75034,USA, https://www.insight.org/resources/bible/the-general-epistles/Hebrews, (September 21, 2018)

About the Author

Mr. Burns received a B.A Bachelor of Architecture from the University of Kentucky in Lexington KY, and a Master of Science in Interior Design from UNCG in Greensboro. Herb has over 39 years' experience in education at Forsyth Technical Community College and has also served as an adjunct faculty at UNCG and Salem College in the Interior Design Departments.

He has received numerous awards for excellence in teaching, and leadership in education and technology. As an educator he has created and taught over a dozen new courses relating to architecture, animation and digital design, and is recognized as an innovator in this field. He is a licensed architect in the State of North Carolina. His knowledge and skills are also known internationally as a guest lecturer on digital design, architecture, sustainability, and best business practices in Finland, Belarus, Russia, and Ukraine. Mr. Burns was also a Fulbright Scholar. He was a member of the first U.S. Delegation to complete a certificate of training in Russian business, law, culture, and economics at the Gazprom College of Oil and Gas Volgograd, Russia.

Mr. Burns has many years of excellent business and executive experiences in Architecture, Computer Aided Design, and Manufacturing. He is a founding collaborator of the Center for Design Innovation, Piedmont Triad Design Consortium, founding collaborator of Design Leadershop, and past president of ABRO Winston-Salem.

Mr. Burns has served as Interim Dean of Engineering at Forsyth Technical Community College, also as the Department Chair for Design Technologies, which includes programs of study in Architecture, Interior Design, Radio and Television and Digital Effects & Animation, and was the Program Coordinator for the

Digital Effects & Animation Program. He also served as the Coordinator of International Partnerships.

Mr. Burns is president of HB Studios, which includes architectural and interior design, digital content, publishing, International, business and educational consulting. https://hibssb.myportfolio.com . Mr. Burns is a host on the podcast series, "Three Men for Thee". https://3-mft.fireside.fm

Purchase your copy of Route 66 at:
https://store.bookbaby.com/book/Route-66
To order large prints 13"x19" or 24"x36",
or
To schedule a speaking engagement email:
HerbBurns@mail.com